Take Charge
Of your

FAMILY

BUSINESS

...Particularly in Difficult Times

S. A. KRISHNAN

Dedicated with Love to my wife Lakshmi.
But for you, my life has no meaning.

FOREWORD 1

INTRODUCTION 3

BASICS OF FAMILY MANAGED BUSINESS 9

REMEMBER WHAT WE ARE TOGETHER FOR: 15

THE PLAN: DO NOT OVERLOOK DETAILS 23

FREQUENT REVIEW 29

HOLD NO SECRETS 31

THE ORGANIZATION MUST OUTLAST YOU 37

KNOWLEDGE IS THE KEY 49

LOOK FURTHER 57

BE A GOOD CORPORATE CITIZEN 63

RELATIONSHIP ISSUES 67

A LOOK AT RATIOS 81

A SURVEY OF FAMILY BUSINESS 105

DETAILS OF THE RESPONSES 107

Foreword

Family Managed Businesses (FMB) have been around for several hundred years and are often the backbone of a nation's economy. A majority of mega-corporations have their beginnings as small FMBs. Yet, while management education and research have done yeomen service to business and the way they should be run, the focus has been on educating managers for the task of and participating in the operation of large public corporations

This booklet aims to educate and inform the reader on the basics of managing an FMB. While it discusses the various tools and techniques, it is written in a style that is easy to comprehend and does not require formal knowledge of or training in business management. In today's environment, a significant number are educated in a general way and some even possess technical qualifications and of course have the entrepreneurial urge. Yet, they lack management skills or do not have formal training in business management. To compound matters, many do not have the time to attend formal classes.

Mr. Krishnan, who has spent several years at senior levels in family business, has attempted to highlight the key areas for managing an FMB. The various concepts, issues and the required tools are spelt out with considerable clarity. And, being a short booklet, entrepreneurs who are hard pressed for time will find it very useful: a good addition for reading as well as reference.

Dr. M.L. Shrikant, D.B.A. (Harvard)
Hon. Dean
S.P.Jain Institute of Management and Research
Mumbai, India

Introduction

A great majority of trade and commerce has been through businesses owned by individuals and families with a large portion being managed by the members of the family. Though no clear data is available on their share, estimates vary that about 90 percent of all U.S. businesses are family owned or controlled while 80 percent of European companies are family managed and in China (including Hong Kong) family managed businesses account for sixty percent and in India it is about 75%. They range in size from the traditional small business, frequently referred to as mom-and-pop establishments, to a little over a third of the Fortune 500 firms. State controlled economies account for a relatively small proportion of entrepreneurs. Nevertheless, even sixty percent is large enough to warrant serious attention.

The smallest of Family Managed Businesses (FMBs) include

petty shopkeepers, mom-and-pop stores, and small professional service providers and so on. The owner is the key person usually aided by one or more assistants. At the other end of the spectrum, there are giant conglomerates with turnover in billions of dollars and employing many thousands at various levels of the organization. In such large organizations, the majority of the employees find no differentiating factor separating the FMB from other types of organizations. It is only at the very top management levels that differences become visible not merely in terms of the style of management but also in matters of reporting, checks and balances and indeed decision making. In its simplest form, the FMB appears to senior managers as one where the roles of the Chief Executive Officer (CEO) and the Board Chairman are combined and where – quite unlike other corporations – most of the key top managers are related to each other.

The world is currently going through a phase of severe recession that has engulfed both the rich as well as the not-so-rich nations. Most developed countries are witnessing a shrinking economy, persistent stories of companies folding up with unceasing regularity, unemployment levels are horrifyingly high and family lives have been badly affected. Much like a poor man does not have much to lose since in any case he does not have any, the lesser developed countries including large ones like China, India and Brazil have been less impacted. These economies too witness slowing down but not a recession in its true economic sense.

The causes for the slowdown – the worst in half a Century – have been debated. Almost any one and every one has an opinion to offer. The reasons attributed vary from recklessly high deficits that countries like USA indulged in, to the greed of bankers and businessmen, to the natural slowing of a over heated economy, the avarice of the unionized labor and so on. Some are resigned to the belief that economic cycles take place with unfailing regularity and very little can be done about them except that steps must be taken by the State for alleviating the distressed.

This downturn in business scenario has hit FMBs hard. It would not be out of place to say that the FMBs are hit harder than other forms of businesses. Indeed, for reasons both logical as well as emotional, many large institutions – notably in the financial sector – and corporations have received considerable bail-out packages from the State. Some have been helped to protect the cause of the labor force while tottering banks have been provided with crutches to ensure that defaulting borrowers get a second chance with life and do not have to be rendered bankrupt. The benefits, efficacy and method of State support will continue to be debated long after the recession is behind us, hopefully in a few years.

The need for the owners of FMBs to take special measures to protect their businesses from the whirlwind of slowdown has become urgent. Just as individuals and institutions build their reputation by consistent and long years of toil and virtuous and ethical actions but can lose them by a mere one false step, so with the FMB as well. Decades of painstaking work that involves building the business brick by brick can all be lost by one wrong step or even by indifference to the recession that is sweeping the world economy.

Unlike large financial institutions where the State feels compelled to intervene for the sake of protecting its clients and indeed to give a push to the economic activity – and offers bail out packages, whether rightly or otherwise - FMBs have no recourse to such succor. After all the State has a two-reason theory: one, it must protect the under privileged (and a few lobbies!) and must restart the economic cycle of activity that has either slowed considerably or has stopped in its entirety. For obvious reasons, an FMB does not fall in this category. One could say that large FMBs have labor force that could clamor for protection. But that is not reason enough. In a free economy like the USA, the way out would be to either rebuild the business or sell out to a potential buyer. Of course, in a socialistic oriented country like those in Europe, the labor protection argument does find favor. It is partly for this reason that, say, Germany offers an incentive for buying a new car though the ostensible reason put forth is to kick-start the economy.

The issues discussed have been written in a simple and easily understandable manner to help assimilation and, more importantly, identifying with the business without taking away the seriousness of the subject matter.

Basics of Family Managed Business

Much like any other, a family managed business (FMB) operates on the broad principles of economics, trade as well as legal and social environment. In that sense it works like any other form of business enterprise with its share of opportunities, problems, competitive areas, business plans, limitations and survival related issues.

One may then ask as what is different and why does it call for special attention and differentiation. The answer can be found in the name.

First, as we have noted earlier, it is a business. Hence most, if not all, business rules, management principles and planning models will apply.

FMBs require the three elements of capital, labor and land as enunciated in the century old work of Alfred Marshall (1842 – 1924) titled *Principles of Economics*. They require too a management team (even if it be just one manager), a product or service that is on offer   and, of course, customer. Any FMB has to operate among these factors and these interact with the business as well as among themselves.

The *second feature* is that of management. As the name suggests, the family that has set up the enterprise manages an FMB. In other words <u>the owner manages and steers the day-to-day operations</u>. He is the CEO and the ultimate authority on decision-making. All risks and rewards stop with him. We use the term "he" but it could be a woman. In fact, as the business grows, it is not just one man or a woman, but a number of members in the family will participate in accepting risks and responsibilities and will take all the key decisions.

It would now be obvious that the two key elements are

"business" and "the family". No matter the size, the reach or the complexity, the two elements of business and family remain central. In a typical mom-and-pop store the family may carry out every aspect of the business. At the other end, one could have thousands of managers at various levels. Yet, in both cases – and many in-between sizes – the family must manage the business. The family's performance determines the business' success or failure.

A question that may arise: would not all businesses be like this? Not quite so. A closer look will show that in many companies, we have an owner, a family that owns or maybe a set of owners. These men and women provide the capital and even have the last say. However, they do not take an active day-to-day interest preferring instead to periodically review progress and problems. It would be similar, though not exactly akin, to a Board of Directors who meets, say, every quarter to take on note the company's performance and give broad guidelines.

Direct day-to-day hands-on management by the owner(s) is the key differentiator of an FMB from other forms of business.

In regard to management of an FMB, the late Peter Drucker, considered as one of the greatest of management *gurus*, there is really no difference between professional management and family-managed businesses when it comes to functional work. On the other hand, when it comes to management of the family business, different rules are required.

Drucker believed that family members should not be allowed to hold positions of significant responsibility unless they are as capable as non-family employees: they should only be allowed to stay in the business if they qualify on merit, not because they are family members. However, in real life this is difficult to put into practice. An entrepreneur or his/her scion believes that he/she is supremely capable of managing the family's firm. There is real ego massaging fun in being the CEO even if that position comes with its own share of tension and, at times, a sense of helplessness.

Respect is a critical dimension of the family member working in the business. If the family member does not command professional respect, they should not be in the company. The major issue: Lack of respect.

A family member who is not willing to work, no matter what their educational background and capabilities, should not be allowed in the family business. Also, if the family member is not of top-management caliber, with the potential to take over leadership of the company, they should actually be paid a stipend to stay away from the business. Some analysts also suggest that family members not be allowed into entry-level positions. Ideally, they should have spent several years gaining practical experience working in another business before joining the family firm.

With regard to promotions, family members should never be given preference if there is a more qualified and better performing non-family member in management. Finally, over time, family members will elect not to enter the business and the company will eventually become totally professionally managed by non-family members.

Drucker believed that," There is little doubt that beyond a certain size, a business can no longer reserve management to family members and remain viable. Beyond a certain size, that management burden increasingly has to be borne by professional managers." Luckily, as FMBs grow in size, they eventually identify and recruit non-family professionals to take up major functions while holding the final say with them. Does that automatically make them competent? The answer is a definite "no". If a large FMB is to succeed and grow, either the owner-CEO is competent or lets the non family Directors and employees take the major decisions. Failing this, there is only one way-down!

Remember what we are together for:

Mission and Vision

Most entrepreneurs start with a hazy idea but with a lot of enthusiasm and determination. Not merely the diamond seekers of the seventeenth century Africa or the gold diggers in North America or, more recently, the myriad men and women who joined the dot com bandwagon, every businessman or woman has stars in the eyes, a vague notion of what they wish to produce and armed with the finances to start the operations.

Surprisingly, every one of the entrepreneurs believes that he has a fail-safe project idea and a detailed plan of execution. In reality this is far from the truth. If they were to ask a trusted friend (or better still a family member) to question them on the details, most will not pass even the second level of analysis leave alone a close examination. We will come to this later.

For starters, one must articulate the Mission and Vision of the business and the family behind it.

A **Mission Statement** defines the purpose of the organization and its principal objectives. Its principal audience is its employees and owners (where the Company is, say, listed and thus has owners outside of the Family as well).

A **Vision Statement** goes beyond the immediate purpose and is generally the articulation of the main promoter's (in our case, the Family) hope and Vision for the business and what the Family seeks to build. Consequently, its audience is universal and frequently goes much beyond the Company itself. For instance, a Family that gets into the businesses of soft drinks and consumer staples could have a Mission Statement for each of the two lines of businesses but a single Vision Statement outlining what the promoter(s) intends to achieve. On occasions, the Vision Statement also indicates the values that the Family wishes to inculcate in their business.

A **Mission Statement** outlines the purpose of the Company. It is a short and succinct way of espousing what it intends to do or achieve. It should be clear, concise and vivid. Some believe that the Mission Statement must be inspiring as well. There is no hard and fast rule in making a Mission Statement as long as it articulates what the firm is all about and it shows clarity. Moreover, remember not to use jargon. Leave that to the advertisement department!

A few examples of Mission Statement are mentioned below.

- The business of manufacturing and maintaining

telecommunication equipments,

- Providing reliable cleaning of homes and offices,

- Publishing and disseminating print and electronic media related to construction industry,

- Offering world class entertainment electronics to a wide spectrum of users,

- Build superior homes for the community while maintaining high standards of ethics and ensuring a clean and safe environment.

- Manufacture toys that are safe, clean and environment-friendly.

- At **IBM,** we strive to lead in the invention, development and manufacture of the industry's most advanced information technologies, including computer systems, software, storage systems and microelectronics. We translate these advanced technologies into value for our customers through our professional solutions, services and consulting businesses worldwide.

- We sell high quality food and beverage products **(Pepsi)**

- **Google**'s mission is to organize the world's information and make it universally accessible and useful (Google)

- **Wal-Mart**'s mission is to help people save money so they can live better.

Note the key words in each of the above examples. In the first, the key words are manufacturing, maintenance and telecommunication while in the second these are reliable, homes and offices. Similarly, the key words in the others too are worthy of note. By way of example, the Mission Statements of IBM, Pepsi, Google and Wal-Mart have been indicated above.

The **Vision Statement** goes beyond the immediate purpose. It acts as a peep into the future and into the mind of the Family. Consequently, it is more general, espouses the values and, possibly, the dream of what one hopes to achieve (even if takes more than one generation to reach it). As a result, a Vision Statement tends to appear a bit more general than the Mission Statement.

Here is a look at some Vision Statements:

- To be among the world leaders in publishing business and maintain an unwavering commitment to ethics, truth and neutrality. Our overall aspiration is to become the most admired business software and services provider in the world.

- At **Alcoa**, our vision is to be the best company in the world--in the eyes of our customers, shareholders, communities and people. We expect and demand the best we have to offer by always keeping Alcoa's values top of mind.

- **(Heinz)** Our VISION, quite simply, is to be "THE WORLD'S PREMIER FOOD COMPANY, OFFERING

NUTRITIOUS, SUPERIOR TASTING FOODS TO PEOPLE EVERYWHERE." Being the premier food company does not mean being the biggest but it does mean being the best in terms of consumer value, customer service, employee talent, and consistent and predictable growth. We are well on our way to realizing this Vision but there is more we must do to fully achieve it.

- **(Pfizer)** We will become the world's most valued company to patients, customers, colleagues, investors, business partners, and the communities where we work and live.

- **(Intel** calls it Mission) Delight our customers, employees, and shareholders by relentlessly delivering the platform and technology advancements that become essential to the way we work and live.

While the companies mentioned above are very large ones, the point to note that they had the vision on their radar for a long time.

21

To recapitulate, a Mission Statement tells what the business is about while the Vision Statement brings out the dream, the ethos and the values treasured by the entrepreneur.

Both the Mission Statement and the Vision Statement must be drafted with care keeping in mind the target audience, clarity of wording, the key aspects sought to be brought-out and be concise.

The Plan: Do not overlook details

A Business Plan is a very important part of starting and running of a business. Sadly, it is given only a passing-look by most entrepreneurs. More often than not many a business has failed just because there was no plan and hence actions – albeit being sincere and good – went awry.

It is often believed – and wrongly too – that a business plan is needed only to approach a financier: and that when an entrepreneur decides to use his/her own funds, such plans are a waste of time! It is very true that a banker or any other financier will like to see a plan so as to understand what the business is about and to evaluate the chances that the operations would succeed thereby ensuring that the money he lends or invests in is quite safe and will yield acceptable returns.

Keys to a good business plan

A good business plan must set concrete goals, responsibilities, and deadlines to guide your business.

It should assign tasks to people or departments and sets milestones and deadlines for tracking implementation.

The plan must be simple, easy to understand and must be practical.

A good plan must address all the components such as the process, the market, the limitations, finances, profitability etc. No aspect should be ignored.

As part of the implementation, it should provide a forum for regular review and course corrections.

Writing a plan

Contrary to some apprehensions, writing a business plan is

not very difficult – and there are enough sample-plans available in library books and on the ubiquitous Internet. These would give one the contents of a plan and some insight into the pitfalls to be avoided.

A typical plan would have the following:

- What the plan is about
  - o Mission
  - o Keys to Success: these would include
- A high level of quality in its product line
- Maintaining and growing its referral networks to generate new and repeat sales
- Significant investments in research and development and engineering with the aim to focus on precisely controlled equipment.
- Improving efficiencies of operations

- Company Summary

  - Company Ownership

  - Start-up Summary

- Product and Market

  - Industry Analysis

  - Market Segmentation

  - Target Market Segment Strategy

  - Market Needs

  - Competition and Buying Patterns

  - Sales forecast

- Human Resources

  - Detailed staff costs

  - Recruitment needs and cost

  - Training needs and costs

- Financial Plan

  - Important Assumptions

  - Break-even Analysis

- o Projected Profit and Loss

- o Balance Sheet

- o Key Ratios

- o Cash Flow: This should include

    - ▪ Periodic estimate of cash flows

    - ▪ Estimation of Capital equipment needs

Stick to the Plan

A Plan is only good if it is followed, reviewed and course correction made. Far too many entrepreneurs fail in implementing the plan. Quite a few believe – and sadly wrongly – that a Plan, once made, will work by itself: far from it. A Plan needs to be continually monitored. That calls for commitment starting from the highest levels. The entrepreneur must also extract commitment at all levels particularly from key employees. To ensure it, the Plan must not only be clear and specific but also easily understandable. To borrow an expression from the famous poet John Milton, it must not only be right but *appear* right.

A good Plan must indicate a modicum of extra effort needed by the people in the organization. Yet, it must appear achievable. If the targets are too stiff, people will give up *ab initio*.

Frequent Review

In the earlier pages, we looked at the need for a Plan, the essential requirements of a good one and the suggestion of sticking to the Plan. It is a common failing – but not a difficult one to avoid – treating a Plan as something of an annual ritual.

Many entrepreneurs have told me that they formulated a good Plan using outside help from experts and sincerely stuck to it and yet the outcome was less than satisfactory. Even as fundamental business shifts and a modicum of incompetence are attributable, a simple failing was not to review the Plan.

Just as one compares actual performance with Plan targets, the assumptions and targets themselves need to be reviewed occasionally. This is not to suggest watering down goals or moving milestones further away. The review gives us the opportunity to assess the correctness of the Plan.

A review may be called for when, say,

1. The Plan looks unrealistic not just to the people in the organization but also to the family.

2. Even if the targets are achievable, it will be at the cost of sacrificing management controls on quality, delivery and financial rewards.

3. There is a basic shift in the environment: this could be due to development of new technology causing obsolescence of the current product line, or a change in consumer preferences or even caused by sudden change in the product cycle.

4. There is a new person at the helm such as when the head of the family passes the baton on to a younger member. Each individual has varying competencies and management style (a good organization should not frequently change *its* style of operations for that would create confusion among employees and could even result in changing the very character).

Hold No Secrets

The power of involving everyone

History – both political and corporate – is replete with data and notes to affirm the power of knowledge: and an FMB, being a business, is not immune to this dictum. It is important for the entrepreneur to arm himself with detailed knowledge of the operations and to be aware of the environment such as industry, the market conditions, competition, research on product and statutory developments. After all knowledge is power: and power is needed to back decisions to be implemented.

At the same time, the Owner-CEO must realize that he/she is not merely a CEO but a repository of the faith and hopes of the members of the family. They too have the desire and even the right to know of the operations and the environment. If the CEO, despite good intentions, does not communicate with them it would lead to apprehension that some thing is amiss and eventually lack of trust in him/her.

It is not that every small decision or action needs to be told to every one. Nevertheless all the family members need to be taken into confidence. This could be done at two levels:

1. With family members actively involved in the operations, and

2. With the entire (adult) family

Small FMBs have typically just one family member running the operations. He/she is the CEO and COO rolled into one. Larger ones could have a number of members from the family donning various positions across functions and divisions. In such a scenario the CEO must hold periodic consultations both informally and at formal structured meetings. Such meetings are crucial for the health of the organization. Apart from getting the involvement of the working members – and thereby enhancing their commitment to the business – it helps better decision-making, removes possible apprehensions and frictions and better co-ordination.

The dialogue and communication must be based on <u>three corner stones</u>:

1. Communication must be free and frank among the members but completely confidential outside of their group.

2. The members must trust each other and repose full faith in the CEO.

3. Even if the members have disagreements or arguments in the meeting, once a decision is taken, every one must take ownership of the decision.

To address the issue of effective communication in larger organizations - and especially where there are a large number of owners - some believe that a family council is the answer. A family council typically consists of the members of the family having a stake however small in the business.

The family council can meet periodically say once a Quarter as also whenever the CEO feels the need to meet on a major or pressing issue. Here again the three basic corner stones indicated above are paramount. In addition, it would be advantageous to hold structured meetings. The members must be given adequate notice, provided with detailed agenda and an appropriate place and time-slot must be set apart where one can be free from other distractions. This last aspect may sound trivial but try attending a meeting where the executives are frequently interrupted by operational issues: the result would be obvious.

It would also be advantageous (at least once every six months) if the family members are given the opportunity to bring up issues that concern them provided that they prepare a detailed note on the issue and it is then circulated along with the rest of the agenda. This would give other members enough time to ponder over the subject and thereby make the formal meetings more productive.

An extension of the concept of involving every one is to ensure that the senior management team includes non family members. For instance, if the family members hold the positions of CEO and Chief Financial Officer (CFO), then it may be useful if the Chief Operating Officer (COO) or the Chief Information (Knowledge) Officer is a non-family person. Drucker humorously mentioned that in the Mafia, the second in command to the Godfather, the *consigliere*, is not a member of the family - and may not even be a Sicilian!

To summarize:

- Communicate regularly and frequently with the members of the family

- Hold structured meetings at least twice a year with clear agenda, have enough time for views from all and allow fresh ideas from non-working members.

- Communication must be free and frank; the members must take ownership of all decisions and maintain strict secrecy with outsiders.

- Members must repose full faith in the family member who is in-charge of the day-to-day operations (the CEO).

Organizations that have clarity and transparency among owners tend to be more efficient and are better equipped to successfully withstand adverse times

The Organization Must Outlast You

Importance of Succession Planning

World-over, corporate laws stress the point that a Company (or an incorporated organization) is an entity by itself and is permanent. In other words, its existence is unaffected by change in leadership or the corporation's owners. It is structured to outlast the owners, the employees and even the individual customer. The corporation dies only in case of bankruptcy (akin to serious illness of an individual) or winding-up motion by (substantially) all its members (sounds similar to suicide?).

Two features emanate from this. One, the FMB (Organization) is distinct from its owner(s). Secondly, well-run organizations will eventually outlive its initial owners.

When an entrepreneur sets out to start a business, it is but natural for his FMB operations to reflect his plans and, indeed, his character and approach to a variety of issues. This is perhaps as it should be. Some of it would invariably be reflected in the Mission and Vision Statements. Yet, with the passage of time (and business needs) the organization develops its own character. This is often, though loosely, called Organization Culture. It means that an organization - and willy-nilly its employees - will respond and react to a situation in its own unique way: and the employees are urged to behave in a similar way to a given situation.

Whether it is the reflection of the owner's thoughts or the emergence of an organization culture, it shows that an organization has a character of its own and indeed is an independent entity with its own personality and a mind of its own. It is, thus, all the more essential that the owners appreciate it and work toward nurturing and sustaining the organization even after their time. This is precisely why a succession plan is needed.

Sharma, P., Chrisman, J., Pablo, A., & Chua, J. (Determinants of initial satisfaction with the succession process in family firms: A conceptual model. *Entrepreneurship: Theory and Practice, 25*(3) 17–35, 2001) define the succession process as "the actions and events that lead to the transition of leadership from one family member to another in family firms. The two family members may be part of the nuclear or extended family, and may not belong to the same generation".

As we have observed earlier, smaller organizations – and typically first or second-generation businesses – have one dominant owner along with a few smaller shareholders. The larger ones and particularly if the business was started by more than one family member, multiple persons hold significant percentage of shares in the firm. In either of the situations, one must have a clear and well-communicated plan of succession.

The process of succession must have, in the main, three components. These include

1. A defined plan,

2. A <u>methodology</u> for identifying the successor and

3. The <u>preparing of the incumbent</u> to assume leadership roles.

Each of these is important in that a weakness in any one of the three elements could ruin smooth passing on of the reins of the FMB.

The Succession Plan

There must be a clear and well-defined plan: and it must be approved by all (or at least a great majority of) the owners of the FMB. It should outline the basis, the steps and the time frame for succession. The plan must be prepared, circulated and approved when the incumbent family member in charge is in the prime of his/her position.

Some of the practices that are in vogue are:

Setting a definite age for retirement: this may sound simple but is a very difficult one: Many CEOs would like to die with their boots on and even more so where the CEO is also a major owner of the business. Very few, if any, CEOs depart willingly.

Defining as to who will succeed: Again, this seems very elementary because of "the-son-follows-the-father" pattern. However consider,

1. What if the FMB is owned by more than one person?

2. And if, as in the popular pattern of handing over the reins to the eldest, what role does the younger scion have?

3. Will male and female members have equal opportunity?

Outlining the process of selecting the successor as also the qualifications expected on the person who should become the CEO

To reiterate, the plan must have the approval of the **entire family** failing which bickering is bound to happen.

The Methodology

This is, in a sense, an extension of the succession plan. The owners must define how the successor is to be chosen. It would be useful to have a committee consisting of, say, two family members, the incumbent CEO, and two or three external advisers. The advisers could be Board Members or outside management consultants.

It is usual for the committee to reach a consensus on the features that they are looking in a successor. These would include, but not limited to, ability to lead, a passion for the business of the FMB, the standing of the candidate in terms of gaining the respect of the owners as well as the employees, suitable professional qualification, a basic understanding of the business etc.

This committee should be told of the perimeter conditions (e.g. the CEO to be as far as possible from within the family). Save for this, the committee should be unfettered and their choice must be respected by the family.

Preparing the successor

Modern day business is complex, fiercely competitive and generates substantial expectations from the family, the employees and the society. It is thus necessary to groom and train the incumbent. The actual process will vary from one organization to another. Yet, these should, at the very minimum, include detailed induction into the operations (unless he/she has had a smaller role in the firm), a period of hand holding and, most importantly, the willingness to let him/her commit mistakes particularly early in his/her tenure as the CEO.

In case, the successor has spent some time working in the FMB, the process of induction and initiation are reduced. However, it would be certainly useful for the successor to spend anything between three and six months working along with the existing (and soon-to-retire) CEO.

It would not be out of place to state that most families induct their children into the business at an early age. Where they fail, are in matters of deciding when the baton will pass and to whom.

The role of the family council is to first define the

responsibilities and qualifications required for the successor in terms of knowledge, skills and experience.

Some suggest the following criteria be considered when identifying potential successors:

- Three to five years employment in a job or jobs that have depended on competence, skill, and sustained performance, rather than on family-based relationships. Many also suggest that this experience should have been gained outside of the family business.

- Experience in directing the activities of others.

- Recognition for proven competence on the job. Evidence and ability to manage relationships, both with peers and with supervisors.

- Evidence of the ability and willingness to take initiative on the job.

- Evidence of having been a valued employee with

45

legitimate contributions to make.

Some good practices

Indeed, quite a few forward-looking FMB organizations have put into practice ground rules for ensuring a smooth succession and thereby ensuring the survival of the company. Some of these include,

- Fixing a retirement age for the CEO

- Ensure that the successor CEO spends <u>at least</u> two years in the Company before the reins are handed over to him/her.

- The Chairman of the Company will invariably be a non-family member and will be a person of substantial standing who will command respect of bulk of the employees and in the society.

- The selection of the CEO is by a committee (both Directors and outside management consultants) with a veto power for the Chairman.

- In some companies, the family insists that the members who will work in the Company must undergo formal training either in technology or management skills.

- To ensure that members do not bicker on emoluments, one major business house has a rule that every member who works will get similar emoluments keeping in mind their age; and the retiring CEO will have his emoluments protected for his life.

- Some families have found merit in instituting a Private Trust to hold the family members' interests. This is to ensure that the business survives any pull and pressure to divide the operations. In a global major, the trust can be dissolved only if all the family members desire so, with a further "fencing" by which a Committee consisting of a retired judge, attorney and a management consultant has to ratify the decision of the family.

Knowledge is the Key

Education and Training

For Centuries, business skills were passed down the generation by observation, some hand holding and practice. This was the scene even beyond the industrial revolution that swept Britain in the Seventeenth Century and followed by other countries, first in Europe and later to other parts of the World.

It was only in latter half of the Nineteenth Century – about a hundred and fifty years back – that complexity in business increased significantly and thus came the need for higher education and formal training. The growth of technical institutes, ensuring adherence to accounting principles, attention to finances, increased concern for the employees (what we now refer to as human resources) and the need to scientifically face competition led to the advent of business schools. Later developments include interface with technology, concern for the society and, importantly, the need to institutionalize ethics.

Indeed the proliferating business schools the world-over is a unique phenomenon of the Twentieth Century. These business schools – some would like to call them the MBA factories – have changed the way business is run. So much so, almost two third of the non-technical positions in most industries require either an MBA degree or at least a modicum of exposure to business management skills. The MBA has become a symbol of business excellence, also lately taken the blame for corporate failures and, for some, even the cause of recession!

We also saw the formation of societies to guide and oversee accounting and related matters. These bodies certify the individual of possessing the necessary knowledge to write and supervise books of accounts. There have also been other agencies on secretarial, stock exchange and related matters:

but these are more to be confronted in publicly held corporations. Those FMBs that have significant public holdings – as also the stocks listed on the bourses – would need to pay attention to this aspect.

When the organization seeks a professionally qualified CEO, COO or CFO, the need for formal training of the family members becomes imperative and obvious. As we have seen, the key-differentiating factor of an FMB is that the owner (family member) is actively involved in managing the day-to-day affairs of the corporation.

To enhance the successful operations, every family member involved in the operations must be trained. The training does not guarantee success: the lack of it seriously impedes the growth and may even lead to failure. Training of the family should be at three levels:

One: Every family member must undergo formal education in technical or managerial skills. It could be a degree in engineering, passing of a course in an accounting body or attending a business school.

It would be quite obvious that one cannot be an expert in all areas of operations. However any CEO must have a working knowledge of the different functions such as finance, operations, marketing, procurement, human resource management and social-legal aspects of business. This knowledge can be gained by either pursuing an MBA course and if the person does not have the time for it or is unable to pull himself away from business for longer periods, he/she could take it up in periodic courses. Of course, as seen later in this chapter, there are courses designed for such a situation

Two.   Training specific to the industry in which the FMB operates is not merely useful but also a necessity.

Three. Science and technology are changing at mind-boggling pace. What is current today could become obsolete in as short a time frame as five years. The change is not merely of the product on hand but how it is marketed, the alternate and more efficient ways of producing it and the steps needed to keep competition at bay.

FMB Oriented Course

During the past two decades an interesting development is that of courses - and even entire schools - dedicated to the training of FMB owners. These range from short programs that run for a week to more elaborate ones that last over eighteen months where the student takes time out from his work (of managing his/her business) and attends classes along with others like him/her. Some of these schools have now become so sophisticated that they mimic an MBA without the pressure of job search at the end of the program!

Among the earliest – and perhaps most comprehensive – is the Center for Family Managed Business at the S.P.Jain Institute of Management and Research, Mumbai, India. A brain child of the venerable Dr M.L.Shrikant, the Center addresses itself to educating and guiding young scions of business families to understand the tools of management and apply them in their own business under the guidance and mentoring of a faculty member. Dr Shrikant, a Harvard educated pioneer and one who is synonymous with modern management practices in India, placed considerable emphasis on synthesizing managerial skills with developing a positive influence on the business family.

A typical program is broken into modules of a week of intense course work where the participants are urged to try to put into practice what they learn in the module: this experience is then shared with fellow participants (who are themselves business family scions) and discussed threadbare with the faculty member guiding, monitoring and mentoring the discussions.

Some of these programs also have an industrial tour thrown in to help the (young) participants get a real life feel of successful FMBs. During the tour, the participants visit organizations that have performed well, get a first-hand impression and meet and interact with the teams managing those companies. An organized international visit enhances the knowledge base.

Look Further

The benefit of thinking global

The recession that is upon us has been very painful. Tens of thousands of people have been rendered jobless and new entrants have seen job opportunities vanishing into thin air, as it were. Corporations have seen falling sales and stare at red ink awash all over the Accounts. Governments have tried to step in with fiscal and non-fiscal help, granted massive bail-outs and have committed to spend on socially relevant areas to boost the economy.

While recessions are unavoidable from the viewpoint of the entrepreneur, steps are possible to reduce the pain and lessen the effect of such economic vicissitudes. Moreover, even if we were to accept that recessions do not happen frequently, business downturns happen with unfailing regularity. It is here that thinking beyond the current business and taking a global approach would help.

At this point one must pause and ponder if we are not overdoing the global case. A majority of the FMBs are small operations often confined to a town or, at most, a county. The concept of "global" then seems way beyond their scope. This is very true. Yet, if we were to define "global" as enlarged area of business, the benefit would at once be visible.

An organization sets itself a perimeter within which it operates. Oftentimes the business module within the perimeter faces a downturn. And while the environment can rarely be controlled, an FMB can be ready for it. There are a number of ways that this can be achieved. In essence these fall in two categories:

One, plan and organize the affairs with pessimistic

possibilities. This is not to contradict the power of positive thinking or develop hopelessness or stop being optimistic: far from it. As the old adage goes hope for the best but be prepared for the worst. So it should be for an organization. In all estimation, target setting, drawing up of plans and processes, the entrepreneur must provide for the unforeseen downturn. Yet another dimension would be that in your SWOT (Strengths Weaknesses Opportunities and Threats) analysis, consider market downturn as one of the possible threats.

Secondly, during good years, do not splurge or pull away the profits. Instead, plough back a fair portion. Use the good times to rectify areas that have previously been overlooked - for instance, the inventory management - and prepare yourself for the difficult ones. Far too often, companies think in terms of control and belt-tightening when faced with losses or lower sales. Sure, the latter is left to poor years but the smarter FMB Owner should review control measures when the going is good.

The *third*, and perhaps more important one, is to have a second line of business. Every organization must have at least two lines. The two, or more, need not be of similar size. There is nothing wrong in having just one line but ensure that there is at least one more line, even if it accounts only for fifteen or twenty percent of the total sales volume.

What is essential, though, is that this must be a line that is not affected significantly the downturn in the primary product. For instance, packaging manufacturer could have school stationery such as notebooks as a minor line. Or, a supplier of electrical cables could also deal in non-electrical building materials. When the primary line suffers a set back, the second one would help cover the basic operational expenses. When the first product sees a decline in volume, the FMB could quickly switch its attention to the second one till such time as the first sees an up turn once again. And this is not a theoretical or imaginary situation. Most products have a periodic dips, many items see a sunset when new products suddenly appear on the horizon and some items do suffer from cyclic volume movements. The existence of the second line will soften the impact of downswings and give you the time to tide over it without seriously hurting the company. Undeniably, this strategy might not protect one from a recession such as the one that is currently upon us. However - and thankfully - recessions do not happen either regularly or frequently!

Be a Good Corporate Citizen

Give back to the society

No man is an island: and this applies to every organization as well. Much like other businesses, an FMB operates in a society. It draws its resources from the society, depends on it for its products and services to be marketed to and owes its existence to the very same environment that we often refer to as "society"

Granted this situation, it is quite obvious that an FMB must do what it can to do something for the society. And make no mistake; it is not a favor but the duty of every FMB. The best part of it is that the society does not expect much!

The entrepreneur must ensure that a small fraction of the

income - even as small as a fifth of one percent - is set apart for socially relevant efforts. This should be supplemented by the entrepreneur and his key team members spending time to work for the society that has nurtured and supported them.

The list of what can be done is endless. Some of these could be,

- Supporting the town and municipality in maintaining the place.

- Helping out with financial support to schools, sports activities, libraries

- Arranging cultural and, where permissible, religious programs.

- Taking up work in support of the blind and other disabled people.

- Take up the cause for socially deprived people

- Volunteer to assist the town and county administration both financially and by physical help from the staff of the company.

The list can be endless. Just remember to give back to the society at least a fraction of what you have earned. What applies to any common successful citizen applies to an FMB as well!

Relationship Issues

Between The Family and Family Business

(The following is gleaned from experience in India, which has witnessed the classic transformation of the FMB from a mom-and-pop store to large organizations, some of which have even made it to the Fortune 500 list. The situation may be local but the lessons are universal to the entrepreneur in his/her FMB.)

Family Managed Businesses (FMB) constitute a substantive proportion of industrial activity in India. While authentic data is not available, estimates put it between 60 and 70 percent of the aggregate output: and the percentage is rising. In the US, this is estimated at almost 90 percent. USA as well as Western Europe has witnessed considerable attention to and research on FMBs (in the US they are referred to as family owned businesses). We now have some business schools and consulting firms that provide formal education of family members in the nuances of FMB.

The relationship between an entrepreneur and his/her business is at once complex and one that significantly affects each other. While the issue of relationship is in itself not new or rare, the complexities certainly are: and the growing size of businesses as well as impact of technology only adds to the problems.

In quite a few cases, the members of the entrepreneur's family – who have a stake but do not participate in day-to-day management – complete the third aspect.

There is, thus, interplay among the owner, the family and the business. Each has its goals that are at variance with and at times in conflict with the other. Ownership, governance and management systems of family businesses are interwoven with family and, therefore, are themselves as particular and individual as the families that founded and control them. These family systems are often part and parcel of the functional solutions, not simply part of the problem, at such firms.

A variety of factors affects the relationships. These include financial structure, family creed, conflict resolution, succession planning, wealth preservation, remuneration of working members, rewarding family members who may not be active on day-to-day affairs, strategic planning etc.

Even while not all of these may be equally important and not even entirely applicable to the Indian context, their impact cannot be wished away. And one must remember that this chart is only that of the family. If we are to superimpose that of the organization, the complexity will multiply manifold. The complexity of relationships unfortunately leads to a peculiar habit of ignoring it and hoping that things would resolve themselves by efflux of time; this seldom happens. Quite the contrary, a delay may cause the resolution to become more difficult.

It is a feature of owner-managers that they believe <u>their</u> problems are unique. They are not. Much like universally applicable principles of management, the problems are themselves not unique – only the specific particulars and players are.

The inter-play of various issues is enough material for an entire book. In this note though, we will merely attempt to introduce and make a brief assessment of some of the major ones in the Indian context.

Building a business that lasts

(Organizational goals versus personal needs)

This may appear stark and even strange. Most entrepreneurs start with the proverbial stars in their eyes and wish to create an organization that will last an eternity. However, most owners cannot resist the temptation of making decisions that are aimed at resolving immediate issues without taking into account the longer time-frame impact. Add to this the personal needs of remuneration and better lifestyle that require significant pay-outs from the company that these men and women create. Growth requires capital (or loans) and in view of large withdrawals, the company is forced to leverage itself. It has been observed in various studies that there is a high correlation between low leverage and the ability to withstand the test of time and competition. When we juxtapose this with the entrepreneur's needs, the business suffers. Consequently, the dreams remain just dreams.

Ownership Issues

In India, the traditional Hindu Undivided Family (HUF) ensured that the collective wealth of a family – at least its male members – stayed as a unit. In such a scenario, the *karta* was the head and took all major decisions both in the structure of the business that the HUF owned as well as deciding on the key players. The progressive collapse of the HUF, accelerated by our desire to copy a Western lifestyle model, raises the twin problems of who owns what and who manages which portion of the organization. An inability to resolve these two key questions results in separation.

Succession (and retirement) planning

If there is one issue that an entrepreneur chooses to ignore, it is that of planning for succession. Despite the knowledge that we are all mortals with an unknown yet definite length of life, we cocoon ourselves in the myth that tomorrow will never come. A logical corollary is that when the inevitable happens, we are unprepared. Fortunately though, entrepreneurs have started involving their children in the business – albeit with limited role – with the result that quite often the youngster forces the issue using the family's communication channels. The erosion of the HUF and its rigors also help.

When two family generations begin to talk to each other, they are speaking from different frames of reference. We are all molded by our individual experiences, which color the lenses through which we see the world. In a family controlled enterprise, the senior generation has usually survived more different experiences of all kinds than its progeny, simply by virtue of age. However, the variety of experience is less important than the sharp inter-generational difference in those experiences. The son or daughter, for example, thinks differently, not just because he/she is less experienced with business or life than his/her father or mother, but because this generation looks at the world through a different prism.

One cannot be in both founder-generation and also of the successor generations. They are different realities. Each of these realities has merit and credibility. The challenge is to build common ground between them. Concerted learning, up-to-date skills, and an eagerness to improve on the old ways obviously differ from seasoned experience and wisdom. The younger generation frequently possesses the former and the senior generation has the latter. When the two sets of traits come together in the family firm, a formidable team can be created.

Involving family members in the business

This problem is more prevalent in the western world. In India, most family businesses are small and significant ownership remains with one or two key members who are also active in the affairs. A combination of businesses entering the second generation owners (without split) as also the more recent observation of female members of families getting a stake in the firm but not participating in it, has brought this to the fore. Not too many studies exist on this subject.

A survey done by the author in 2002 in select industrial areas in the Indian States of Maharashtra and Gujarat threw up possible solutions.

The first is that of the need for open and continuous communication with **all** the (family) stake holders. Lack of correct and timely information leads to doubts, apprehension on the wealth and at times even suspicion. Consultations – structured as well as informal – also help.

Clarity of the individual's roles and using the non-involved members as an advisory forum also help matters. The person managing the business must not only be competent but must be seen to be so. As a corollary, positions in the company must be given to people in the family based on merit rather than nearness to the principal shareholder. This is the most difficult issue. At one level, particularly if the CEO is the single largest shareholder, a natural choice accepted by his society is his/her child. In India, even political parties are governed by dynastic tendencies! The problem arises when there is more than one to choose from among the family. Quite a few families have tackled this by taking outside professional help in making the correct choice as also to gain acceptance of the choice among the other family members.

In yet other firms, family commitment was obtained by ensuring that no single individual could make major decisions alone. This is not to be confused with the much criticized committee concept: rather it involves distribution of responsibilities and forcing consultations in small and tight groups often of just two people. The disadvantages of difference of opinions- it seems – is more than offset by willing participation.

Non-family members in management

Growth in size, rapid advancement of technology and geographic dispersion of the business necessitate the introduction of "outsiders" unless, as a senior banker in Switzerland once said, "our expansion is limited as we do not have enough Swiss nationals willing to work outside the country, particularly Asia"!

Non-family members bring the requisite knowledge but will always lack the oneness with the Company. Their commitment can be enhanced by generous and merit based reward mechanism. Larger family businesses also offer small stakes in the business both as a reward as also obtain greater involvement. A spin off benefit of having outsiders in key positions is their ability and availability to train the younger members of the family.

Financial structure

A majority of the companies that were surveyed reveal a simple form of share holding by the entrepreneur or collectively by his immediate family controlling upward of

90% of the capital, the remaining being given to (family) associates and, in a few instances, to friends as well as trusted and long associated employees. Fiscal benefits given to Small Scale Industries (SSI) have spawned a large of number of companies by the same entrepreneur under different family names and often under the same roof. The gradual withdrawal of these fiscal concessions together with clearly perceived benefits of scale for larger companies has led to some mergers.

Families that own large and multiple businesses often have complicated - albeit unnecessary – cross holdings, created mainly by the flow of funds from one company to the other and to a lesser extent as a defense mechanism to ward off predator attacks on the company by a potential competitor.

Conflict Resolution

The substantial holdings help in minimizing possible

conflicts for control. Unlike in the western countries, most conflicts are resolved by protracted negotiations often helped with the presence of a friendly and respected arbitrator. Legal squabbles for control or even division are relatively rare in India.

The way forward

Realization of the need for more research is itself half the battle. The need is for accelerated attention to enhancing the viability, sustainability and most importantly, the raising of efficiency in FMBs is vital. Focused management education is an obvious route. And if we reiterate the fact that FMBs constitute the single largest group in industrial activity, their importance would be better appreciated.

A look at Ratios

This book is not about detailed financial analysis. Yet, Ratios are a vital measure of understanding and control. Putting it another way, they help an entrepreneur to better manage his/her Family Business.

One must remember though, every entrepreneur has his/her own set of financial and physical parameters that are reviewed, compared and analyzed. The physical parameters include production quantities, Dispatch data, employee efficiency, inventory details etc. While entrepreneurs spend considerable time on financial statements, an area that is overlooked is the power of financial ratios which provide timely pointers.

In this light, the following gives a simplified approach to

understanding Ratios. As top management, emphasis should be on broad principles rather than extreme accuracy or (debatable) inclusion/exclusion of specific items in ratios. Accuracy and correctness are important but not to the extent of hair splitting extremes which may make the entire exercise theoretical.

Ratios make meaning only when used as comparisons either with other companies or over different points of time in your own company. Further, ratios are an indicator particularly of areas of concern.

In making comparisons, remember to check that the accounts of both the companies (and/or both time periods) are drawn up similarly. For example, issues like method of depreciation, method of valuation of inventory, whether there are disproportionately large investments or deferred taxes in one company and not in another etc.

And the most important element is to understand as to _what_ the ratio indicates.

By way of illustration, calculations for a well known cement company (GACL) for the years 2005 and 2004 are explained. At the cost of repetition, it must be stated that certain simplistic way of calculations have been done to make it understandable easily even for non-finance entrepreneurs and students. Also, the sequence has been changed to move logically from Debt to Liquidity, then on to Activity (efficiency of asset utilization) and finally to profits and overall performance.

Profit and Loss and Balance Sheet of Ambuja Cements

	2004-2005 Rs. in Crores	2003-2004 Rs. in Crores
INCOME		
Sales	3,025.84	2,301.28
Less : Excise Duty Paid	420.05	335.99
	2,605.79	1,965.29
Other Income	74.57	50.49
	2,680.36	2,015.78
EXPENDITURE		
Manufacturing Expenses	**1,227.93**	891.97
Variation in Stocks	**(6.97)**	(11.27)

Employee's Cost	**105.53**	86.89
Administrative, Selling and Other Expenses	**558.60**	464.57
Interest and Finance Charges (net)	**84.75**	78.43
Depreciation and Amortization	**195.41**	168.61
	2,165.25	1,679.20
Less: Sell consumption of Cement	**3.43**	3.90
	2,161.82	1,675.30
Profit before Tax and Prior Period Items	**518.54**	340.48
Prior Period Items		
Depreciation Written Back	-	60.57
Employee's Cost	-	(1.78)
Administrative, Selling and other Expenses	-	(15.27)
	-	**43.02**
Profit Before Tax	**518.54**	383.50

Provision for Taxation		
-- Current Tax	**39.12**	20.30
-- Deferred Tax (Refer Note 8)	**10.38**	26.41
Fringe benefit Tax	**0.75**	-
	50.25	46.71
Profit after Tax	**468.29**	336.79
Balance as per last account	**117.54**	90.96
Debit Balance of Profit and Loss Account as on 1st June, 2004	**320.90**	-
of erstwhile Ambuja Cement Rajasthan Limited (ACRL	-	320.90
Less Adjusted from General Reserve		320.90
	-	-
Transferred from Debenture Redemption Reserve	**31.25**	127.75
Transferred to Debenture Redemption Reserve	**25.00**	2.55

Transferred to General Reserve	**225.00**	275.00
	367.08	275.95
Interim Dividend on Equity Shares	**108.05**	88.25
Corporate Dividend Tax on above	**15.16**	11.31
	123.21	99.56
Proposed Final Dividend on Equity Shares	**81.11**	53.82
Corporate Dividend Tax on above	**11.38**	7.03
	92.49	60.85
Balance carried to Balance Sheet	**151.38**	117.54
Notes Forming Part of Accounts		
Earnings Per Share in Rs. (Based on Rs 2 per share Refer Note 7)		
Basic	**3.47**	2.83
Diluted	**3.46**	2.63

	As on 30.06.2005 Rs. in Crores	As on 30.06.2004 Rs. in Crores
SOURCES OF FUNDS		
Shareholder's Funds		
Share Capital	**270.38**	179.40
Share Application Money, pending allotment	-	0.02
Employee Stock Option outstanding (Refer Note 20)	**0.03**	0.05
Reserves & Surplus	**1,908.01**	1,842.29
	2,178.42	2,021.76
Loan Funds		
Secured Loans	**549.33**	649.78
Unsecured Loans	**578.12**	619.90
	1,127.45	1,269.68

Deferred Tax Liability,net{Refer Note 8}	381.09	370.71
Total	3,.686.96	3,662.15
APPLICATIONS OF FUNDS		
Fixed Assets		
Gross Block	3,709.17	3,658.07
Less: Depreciation	1,463.93	1,284.14
Net Block	2,245.24	2,373.93
Capital Work in Progress (Refer Note 22)	75.03	101.35
	2,320.27	2,475.28
Advances against Capital Expenditur	43.07	22.94
	2,393.34	2,498.22
Investments	1,125.06	1,010.97
	2498.22	2,012.36
Investments	1,101.97	1,101.71

Current Assets, Loan and Advances		
Inventories	**317.00**	254.28
Sundry Debtors	**45.84**	42.71
Cash and Bank balances	**86.53**	68.83
Other Current Assets	**1.81**	0.74
Loans and Advances	**136.66**	124.80
	587.84	491.36
Less Current Liabilities and Provisions		
Liabilities	**288.79**	275.98
Provisions	**106.77**	71.34
	395.75	347.29
Net Current Assets	**192.09**	144.07
Miscellaneous Expenditure (to the extent nor written off or adjusted)	**6.47**	8.89
Total	**3,686.96**	3,662.15

Notes:
1. Crore refers to ten million.
2. Only the major items are mentioned: schedules have been avoided to reduce clutter and confusion.

RATIOS OF DEBT

$$Debt\ -\ Equity\ Ratio = \frac{Total\ Liabilitieses}{Owners'\ Equity}\ (\%)$$

(Note: Some analysts suggest that only long-term liabilities be considered)

$(1127.45 + 381.09)/2178.42 \quad = 0.692$

$(1269.68 + 370.71)/2021.76 \quad = 0.811$

The Company's debt-equity ratio has reduced in 2005 as compared to 2004. In other words, the Company has used lesser proportion of debt. Usually this is a good sign, but occasionally it could also mean that the Company has not been able to find use for its retained profits and so has resorted to repaying debt.

<u>Significance for an FMB</u>: Good business must have a proper mix of debt and equity. The quantum of debt varies with industry, the reputation of the entrepreneur and the rate of turnover of capital employed. While increased borrowing appears tempting, one should be on guard against the risk of negative cash flow. For instance the lender could recall the loan or there is an unforeseen delay in recovery of receivables. There have been cases of businesses that have collapsed merely because the entrepreneur has over stretched himself. If an entrepreneur chooses not to have any debt, it will cause undue strain on his finances and also result in lower Return on Equity (explained in later pages). Thus, unless there are compelling reasons (such as idle capital), the entrepreneur must have a mix of both debt and equity and periodically keep a watch on this ratio.

$$Interest\ Cover = \frac{Pre\ Tax\ Operating\ Profit + Interest}{Interest} (No.\ of\ Times)$$

$(518.54-74.57+84.75)/84.75 = 6.238$

(383.50-50.49+78.43)/78.43 = 5.246

This indicates an improvement in the ability to service interest. Occasionally bankers try to determine the ratio to include both interest as well as installments due within one year. To do this, add the installments in the denominator. For example, if the installments due are 50 Millions, then the denominator will become 84.75 plus 50.00.

Significance for an FMB: This is more of determining the comfort levels in the operations. Obviously, the higher the ratio the better off that one is. It does not mean that one reaches for the moon. The entrepreneur must ascertain his comfort level and try to maintain this.

$$Debt\ Turnover = \frac{Cash\ Generated\ by\ Operations\ les}{Total\ Debt}\ (\%)$$

548.15/1127.45 = 0.486

482.01/1269.68 = 0.379

This gives two indicators: one, the Company has improved its cash flow movement and two, (probably because it is in a capital intensive business) cash generation in relation to debt is not very large.

RATIOS OF LIQUIDITY

Net Working Capital = Current Assets minus Current Liabilities

587.84 Minus 395.75 = 192.09

491.36 Minus 347.29 = 144.07

This is strictly not a ratio but indicates how much liquidity is left in the company at each year-end. Here again GACL has a better year (2005) as compared to 2004.

$$Current\ Ratio = \frac{Current\ Assets}{Current\ Liabilities}\ (Ratio)$$

587.84/395.75 = 1.485

491.36/347.29 = 1.415

Significance for an FMB: **Current ratio is a very important one.** A ratio of one or higher means that the company is solvent. In rare cases, a very high (say 4:1) may indicate that the company is not able to get good terms from its creditors. A ratio less than one is a cause for concern. Usually it indicates that in an emergency, the company may face liquidity crisis. This often happens when a company borrows short-term loans and uses them for buying fixed assets or making investments outside the company. In our example, the Company has matters under control.

$$Acid\ Test\ Ratio = \frac{Monetary\ Current\ Assets}{Current\ Liabilities}\ (No.of\ Times)$$

Acid Test Ratio (also called the Quick Ratio) is similar to current ratio except that we delete inventory the reason being that it is not possible to dispose off inventory without incurring major loss of value. Similarly it will be useful to exclude advances/ deposits in subsidiaries or government bodies. We have also excluded debts outstanding for more than six months. Consequently, for GACL these would appear as below:

(42.89 + 86.53)/395.75 = 0.327

(39.65 + 68.83)/347.29 = 0.312

RATIOS OF ACTIVITY

$$Asset\ Turnover = \frac{Sales}{Total\ Assets}\ (No.\ of\ Times)$$

2605.79 / 3686.96 = 0.707

1965.29 / 3662.15 = 0.537

This indicates a faster turnover of assets (some what similar to capital employed). A better asset turnover will help in better return on equity as would be seen later in this note.

$$Capital\ Turnover = \frac{Sales}{LongTerm\ Liability + Equity}\ (No.of\ Times)$$

2605.79 / (451.56+488.40+2178.42) = 0.836 times.

1965.29 / (529.78+434.61+2021) = 0.658 times.

Here too GACL has shown a good improvement in using its capital employed in business.

$$Working\ Capital\ Turnover = \frac{Sales}{Working\ Capital}\ (No.\ of\ Times)$$

2605.79 / 192.09 = 13.56 times

1965.29 / 144.07 = 13.64 times

This indicates that there is no major change, possibly because there is not much room for improvement.

$$Capital\ Intensity = \frac{Sales}{Buildings + P\&M + Office\ Equipmt.}\ (No.of\ Times)$$

2605.79 / 2245.24 = 1.16 times

1965.29 / 2373.93 = 0.828 times

The Company has been able to step up its turnover without corresponding increase in fixed assets.

$$Collection\ Period = \frac{Accounts\ Receivables}{Sales\ /\ 365}\ (Days)$$

45.84 / (2605.79/365) = 6.42 days

42.71 / (1965.29/365) = 7.93 days

This means that on an average the Company has a little over six days of receivables. It will make meaning only when compared to competitors. Of course, like the previous ratios, here too GACL has improved on its previous year.

PROFITABILITY RATIOS

$$Gross\,Margin = \frac{Gross\,Margin}{Net\,Sales}\,(\%)$$

For sake of simplicity, we have only taken the major elements in the P&L account.

2605.79 – (1227.93-6.97+105.53+558.60) / 2605.79 = 27.65%

1965.29 – (891.97-11.27+86.89+464.57) / 1965.29 = 27.13%

The Company has been able to maintain its margins intact.

$$Profit\ Margin = \frac{Net\ Profit}{Sales}\ (\%)$$

468.29 / 2605.79 = 17.97%

336.79 / 1965.29 = 17.14%

This shows an improvement over last year.

$$Earnings\ Per\ Share = \frac{Net\ Profit}{Number\ of\ Shares}\ (Dollars)$$

468.29 / 135.18 = dollars 3.463 for a two-dollar share

336.79 / 17.939 = dollars 18.77 for a ten-dollar share or 3. 75 for a two-dollar share.

It must be mentioned that GACL had issued a bonus of 1 for two shares. If this were to be adjusted, then the current year figure shows a sharp improvement over last year (you can either increase the number of shares for previous year or reduce that of current year by the bonus amount, to make a correct comparison).

$$Return\ on\ Assets = \frac{Net\ Profit + Interest\,(1 - Tax\ Rate)}{Total\ Assets}\,(\%)$$

In the calculation below, we have assumed a tax rate of 35%. These ratios can also be calculated without tax rates.

468.29 + 84.75 * (1 – 0.35) / 3686.96 = 14.19%

336.79 + 78.43 * (1 – 0.35) / 3662.15 = 10.59%

Note the sharp jump in the above.

Return on Capital Employed (RCE)

$$RCE = \frac{Net\ Profit + Interest\ (1 - Tax\ Rate)}{Long\ Term\ Liab. + Owners'\ Equity}\,(\%)$$

468.29 + 84.75 * (1 − 0.35) / (451.56 + 488.40 + 2178.42) = 16.78%

336.79 + 78.43 * (1 − 0.35) /(529.78 + 434.61 + 2021.76) = 12.98%

Significance for an FMB: The end purpose of most businesses is to generate an acceptable return on resources employed. The entrepreneur must aim for a minimum rate of return below which serious concerns must be raised. Whenever this ratio is breached downward, it is a caution signal requiring urgent attention.

$$\textbf{\textit{Return on Equity}} = \frac{\textbf{\textit{Net Profit}}}{\textbf{\textit{Owner's Equity}}}\textbf{\textit{(\%)}}$$

468.29 / 2178.42 = 21.497%

336.79 / 2021.76 = 16.658%

We will examine this again in some detail.

A COMPARISON WITH ACC

Given below is a comparison of some ratios with that of industry leader ACC.

	GACL		ACC	
	2003-04	2004-05	2003-04	2004-05
Current Ratio	1.415	1.485	1.222	1.187
Asset Turnover	0.537	0.707	1.069	1.147
Equity Multiplier	1.811	1.692	2.269	2.128
Profit Margin	17.14%	17.97%	6.09%	9.69%
Return on Cap Employed	12.98%	16.78%	7.55%	12.37%
Return on Equity	16.66%	21.50%	14.77%	26.65%

It would be seen that both GACL and ACC have shown improvements over the previous year. Profit margins at GACL are distinctly higher. But ACC has a better Asset Turnover as well as higher Equity Multiplier. This means that even with a small increase in profit margin, ACC can sharply raise its ROE.

Return on Equity

We have observed in the earlier pages that Return on Equity is the ratio of Net Profit to Owner's Equity (capital). Now consider the ratios given below (we have already seen the first two earlier)

1. Net Profit Margin which we have seen as "Net Profit / Sales"

2. Asset Turnover which is expressed as "Sales / Assets", and

3. Equity Multiplier which can be expressed as "Assets / Equity"

If we multiply all the three, we will be left with "Net Profit / Equity" which is nothing but Return on (owner's) Equity.

While the need for a good profit margin seems obvious, note the importance of asset turnover and the need to keep a watch on how rapidly the equity is turned over by its assets. *It would become clear that the greater the ratio of assets to the company's equity, the better would be its ROE.*

A Survey of Family Business

Summary of Major Findings

The target respondents were **firms that were owned <u>AND</u> actively managed by the family(ies)** that own them. The details of the responses are given in some detail in the next section.

- We received 171 responses from about four hundred mailers

- As many as 74 responses were from the Western States, with 31 from North, 49 from South and 17 from the East

- The average was an asset size of $950,000 and with 36 employees; predominantly in manufacturing and having a single product line

- The FMB Heads had a reasonable level of education

- The majority are first generation entrepreneurs with

only about 10% being third generation

- The management in most cases was a "one man" show despite claims of consensus etc

- Very few had any real plans of succession planning. Even more importantly– and perhaps unfortunately – this did not appear to be a serious issue.

- A little over 20% of the respondents had women family members in active positions

- The respondents claimed a fairly high degree of communication among the family members though this claim may NOT be accurate

- Most did not seek external help in strategy etc; in most cases it was related to consulting the auditor ostensibly for tax matters

- There appears to be confusion between long term goals and short term ones: <u>year-on-year growth seemed to be the most important aim.</u>

Details of the Responses

General Profile

Number of years in this business:

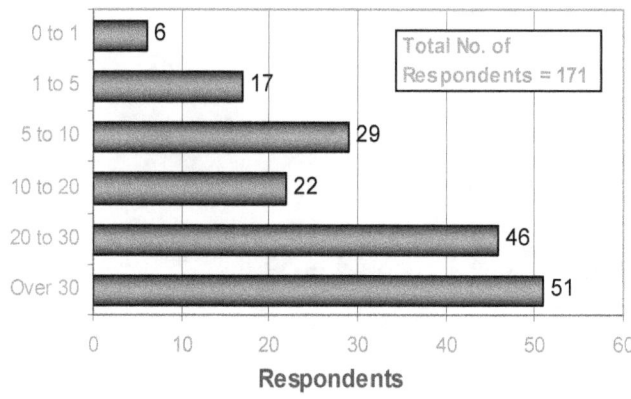

Number of Years in this Business

Total No. of
Respondents = 171

0 to 1	6
1 to 5	17
5 to 10	29
10 to 20	22
20 to 30	46
Over 30	51

Respondents (0, 10, 20, 30, 40, 50, 60)

The oldest firm was little over 108 years old.

Number of Employees

The average number of employees was 36.

Purchased or started:

Purchased or Started?

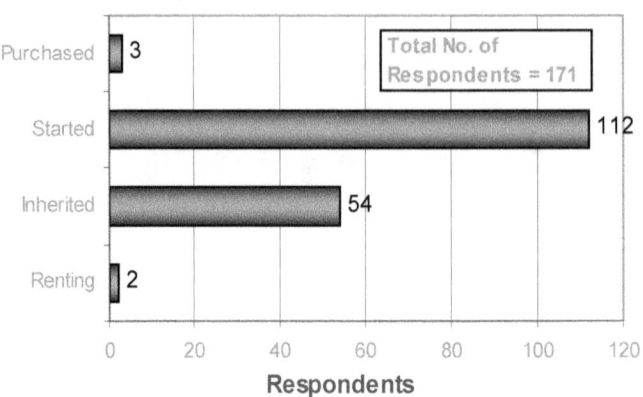

Ownership

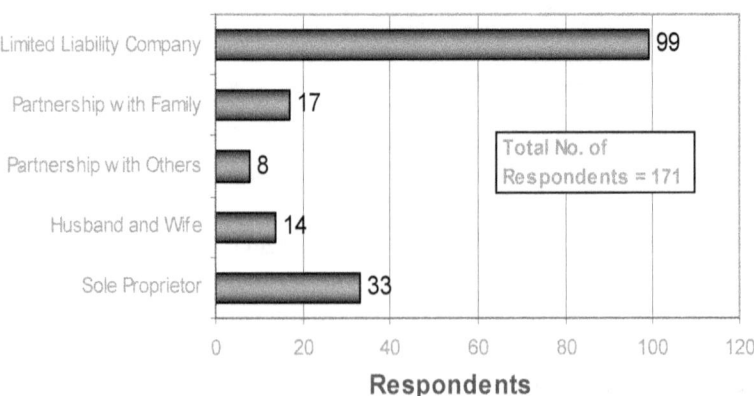

As many as 115 respondents claimed that they (and in some cases along with their wife) are the principal owners. As for

108

the others,

- One/Two   21
- Three/Four   13
- Four/Five   18
- Over Five   4

How many of above participate in day-to-day affairs of the business?

The average number was two (usually father/son, husband/wife or two or more brothers). 67 respondents indicated only one active member. 32 mentioned two and the balance three or more.

Number of Paid employees (Non Family Members):

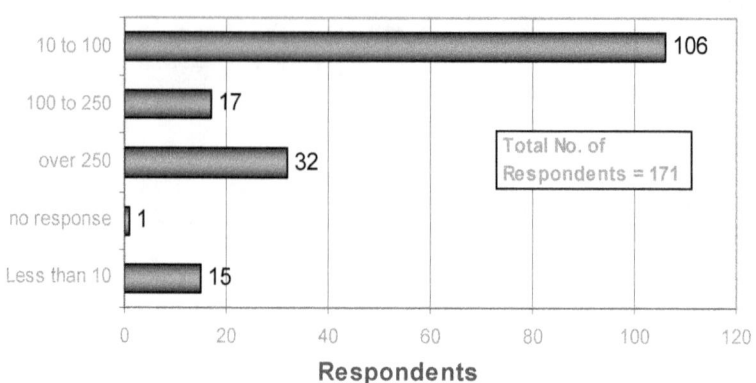

Non-Family Members Full Time

Category	Respondents
10 to 100	106
100 to 250	17
over 250	32
no response	1
Less than 10	15

Total No. of Respondents = 171

Education

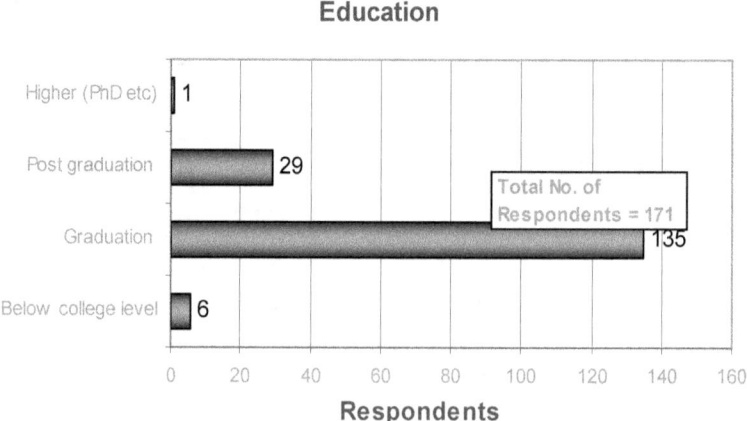

Education

Category	Respondents
Higher (PhD etc)	1
Post graduation	29
Graduation	135
Below college level	6

Total No. of Respondents = 171

Previous business ownership

110

Previous Business Ownership

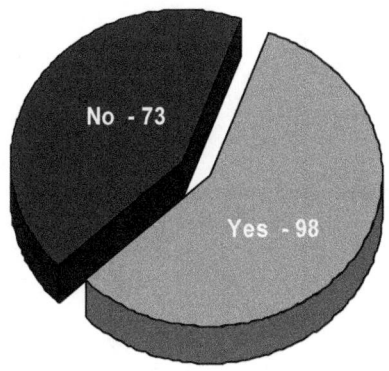

Extent of family involvement:

- No other family member(s) beside me 102

- A husband and wife work together   17

- One or more of the owner's children work here   41

- Other family members involved   11

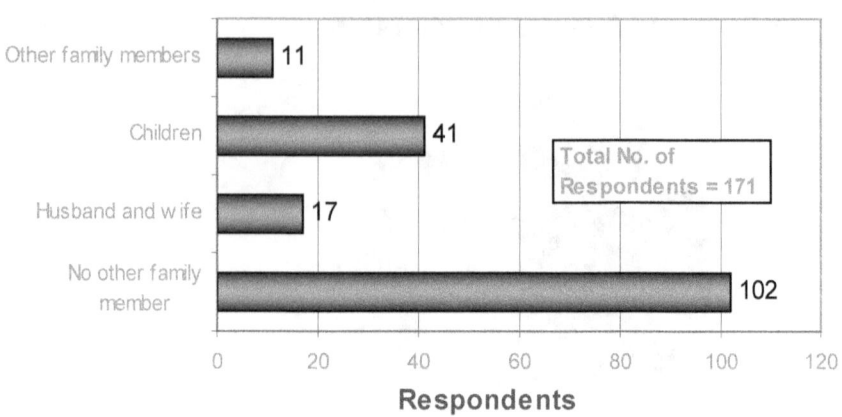

Family Involvement

Other family members — 11

Children — 41

Husband and wife — 17

No other family member — 102

Total No. of Respondents = 171

Respondents

Do you have a succession plan in place?

Succession Plan

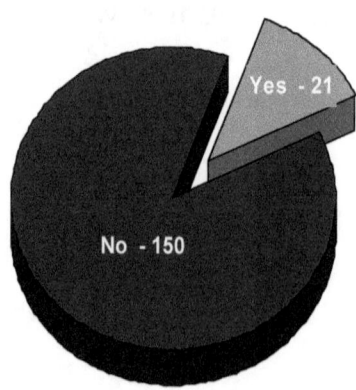

Yes - 21

No - 150

If you want your children to inherit your business, would there be a problem?

This question was not answered properly. Most respondents stated that their children would be happy to take over their business.

Eleven respondents stated that their children did not wish to remain in "low tech" business while nine indicated that their children wished to settle overseas.

Disposition Plans:

Here again, the respondents were evasive or unclear. Most of them stated that their business would go to their wife/child and it is up to them to deal suitably. Two respondents, though, had ideas of transferring the business to a Trust so that the profits could be used for charity. One of these two had no children while the other and his wife believe that they must give back to the society what they have earned and hence will bequeath only a small fraction to their child and give away the rest to charity.

Analyzing the Business

Q. How many generations of the family (or families) have been involved in the operation of this firm? (Include any retired or deceased family members)

· One   86

· Two   68

· Three or more 17

Q. Is at least one founder of the firm still active in the management of the firm?

Yes   109

No   62

Q. Are any of the firm's higher-level managers non-family members?

Yes 86

No   85

Q. How many "higher-level managers" does the firm have in the aggregate? How many of these are non-family members?

A. Most responses indicated 1 to 3 senior positions. Fourteen responses had 4 to 6 while two (large firms) indicated over 6.

Women in the family business: Only 36 firms had active involvement of women family members but many said that this was because their wives did not have the time. Over a hundred replies stated that if necessary their wives would be involved. Mention was made by seven that when their daughters grew up, they would don the business mantle.

Q. Involving most, if not all, family members in important management decisions (on a scale of 1 to 7):

A. The median was 4.5 with 9 replies calling it very important and just 1 reply stating that all decisions are made solely by one person only.

Q. Conflict among family members:

A. Most replies were between 3 and 1, indicating minimal conflict. Two respondents circled 6

Q. Regular communication among family members

 A. 165 replies circled 6 (high level of communication), two circled 5 and four circled 1

Q. Succession Plans:

A. 117 respondents circled 6 (good plan exists), 31 circled 5 and the remaining circled 2 or did not reply.

Q. Use of outside consultants, advisors and professionals services.

A. Most respondents were vague, though three indicated that they have an outside consultant while at least twenty five others indicated their intention of appointing one.

Time spent on planning and long-term direction of the business: Though other responses did not match with this, nevertheless, as many as 152 believed that they dwelt at length on future planning and only four indicated inadequacy.

Q. Use of sophisticated methods of financial management (such as capital budgeting, breakeven analysis, discounted cash flow, sales forecasting etc)

A. 37 believed they use sophisticated tools, 128 circled either 4 or 3, while the balance were either unclear or did not believe in such concepts.

Q. The original business objectives and methods of the founder (or founders) of this firm continues to strongly influence current top management styles and decisions.

A. 136 respondents said that the original aims are in place, 23 ticked 4 while the remaining either ticked 1 or stated that the firm has undergone a lot of change. One respondent said that only the name remained unchanged: everything else including the product and the guiding philosophy had changed even while the firm remained in the hands of the founding family.

Going Public: Barring seven, all said that they are either public or will do so at an early opportune moment.

Q. This firm's top management style is:

Formal, objective, non-paternalistic 7 6 5 4 3 2 1 informal, subjective, paternalistic

A. 165 respondents circled 7 (but quite a few added comments that their firm was very warm and understanding toward their employees), one circled 5, and five circled 2.

Q. Which source of financing provided in the greatest

amount of funds in the past five years?

Debt -----loans, cash advance, credit cards etc.

Equity ---- sales of stock , new partners , personal savings etc.

A. The median debt to equity was 1.7. Four respondents stated that they would not   borrow while three stated that they would leverage to the best extent possible.

Q. Which category best describes this firm's industry?

Product ---- manufacturing etc.   126

Service ---- retail, business services , etc.   45

Plans and Strategies

The Numbers

The average asset (without revaluation) was 42 million with 375 million and 1.1 million being the extremes. The owners' equity (including re-investments) was just under 26 million.

As many as 126 had a single product, 39 had two and the remaining mentioned three or more.

Almost all respondents said that one product contributed to most of the revenue and profits.

Only 26 respondents claimed a written business plan (and some of these claimed that it had been approved by the key family members). About 30 indicated that there was some recorded document on the plan while the majority stated that business plan was known to the family though not recorded in the orthodox sense.

(Not unexpectedly) most respondents claimed that their goal was to grow and to be a responsible organization. The entrepreneurs desired consistent growth, maintaining profitability and, in three cases, sought to be the market leader.

Seventeen respondents indicated consensus (among

family members), 114 indicated that the FMB head took all the decisions while the remaining were unclear. Some of the respondents spoke of keeping pace with recent technology, four mentioned the need to keep a watch on possible obsolescence and 36 mentioned aggressive posturing. (It was obvious that the respondents did not quite understand the question: perhaps it should have been worded better).

Almost all the respondents indicated their need for debt though in varying proportions. As mentioned in an earlier question, four did not want debt. As to the Capital, three indicated going public within the next two years, seventeen indicated looking for equity from extended family members (though they should not interfere in the management, as some put it) and 135 said that in the future they would seek external capital.

Most respondents said that they consult their auditor, (in some cases) a specialist adviser, family patriarch etc.

Interestingly there was no consultation in the community as far as business strategy was concerned.

As many as 136 respondents answered in the negative, 27 said that community members were happy to participate in the capital if invited, 6 mentioned actively wooing the community and one respondent said "he could not care less".

Practically all the respondents stated that the key working member(s) decided on the remuneration of other working family members. Annual review was the dominant frequency. Two respondents indicated half-yearly and eight mentioned that it is done once in two years (with annual increase at predetermined steps).

Remuneration of non family members in senior positions was either market oriented or, in a few cases, ad hoc.

Remuneration of family members was NOT related to profits. A few indicated that in "good" years the family members tended to splurge a bit more.

For family members, there appears to be no retirement date and is left to the individual as to when to hang up his boots. About a dozen did mention that senior family members did indicate about two years ahead of their plan to retire thus making it easier for the planning of succession.

In regard to ownership, (1% or more) the median figure was just over 6. Seven respondents indicated over 10, eighty-three mentioned 7, sixty five entrepreneurs quoted between 6 and 4 stake holders and the remaining less than three.

As for non family members, ownership was negligible. Three respondents wrote about a large number of employees and friends but very few holding over a percent. <u>Clearly the FMB owners were apprehensive in sharing ownership with outsiders.</u>

Most replies indicated quarterly reporting as the favored time lag. Some mentioned of continuous dialogue while four respondents stated that all the shareholders meet every month albeit informally.

The answer was in the affirmative when it came to non family seniors as well. One must however remember that non-family members rarely had significant holding. At least forty-six respondents said that communication was essentially restricted to principal family members.

Business Strategy

When asked to rank in terms of importance, year-on-year growth was the choice of an overwhelming majority of entrepreneurs.

- Profit   THREE
- Market share   FOUR
- Turnover   TWO
- Year-to-year growth   ONE

- Others   FIVE

As many as 156 respondents did not deem it necessary to compare themselves with competition (surprise!) and yet some of them did mention of "ascertaining" the plans and strategies of competitors

Q. If more than one family member is a major decision maker, how difficult is it to gain mutual acceptance

- Very difficult   17 respondents
- Not so difficult   96
- Do not find it difficult at all   68

Eleven family heads indicated that they would seek professional (read human resources) help from outside while six trusted family meetings to sort out issues. (The expression "family council", which is so common in the west, was conspicuous by its absence with only one mentioning it)

The majority of entrepreneurs believed that some family member makes efforts to ensure that the strategy decided upon is acceptable to all.

Succession

There were some contradictions in the responses. The impression gathered is that most respondents <u>believed</u> that they had succession plans, but only 37 indicated any clear ideas. As many as 21 assumed that things would fall in place on their own. Only 28 stated that they had definite ideas of taking professional help.

Growth and managing growth

Not surprisingly, all but one stated that growth was essential and imminent and so were plans. 145 respondents believed that they would grow in the same place, 19 wrote about plans for multiple locations while the remaining 7 were unsure

In case of a need to look for growth in other locations, the response was:

- Another family member   13 respondents
- You will do it yourself   6 respondents

Five of the six above (who planned to do it by themselves) believed in appointing professionals to head the local operations in the new place.

www.ingramcontent.com/pod-product-compliance
Lightning Source LLC
Chambersburg PA
CBHW051541170526
45165CB00002B/821